# How to Spot an Otter

Written by Becca Heddle

## Contents

| | |
|---|---|
| Otters | 2 |
| What do otters look like? | 4 |
| Strong swimmers | 6 |
| Smart hunters | 8 |
| Otter dens | 10 |
| Otter spotting | 12 |
| Otter facts | 14 |

**Collins**

# Otters

Otters are fantastic! They can be hard to spot, but this book will help you to be an otter expert.

# What do otters look like?

Otters are strong and sleek, with thick brown fur.

long, thick tail

little ears

bright and clear

lighter throat

short, strong legs

# Strong swimmers

A good habitat for otters is near rivers or by the coast.

They are expert swimmers.
From when they are ten weeks old,
otter pups can swim!

# Smart hunters

Otters are good at hunting, too. They swim along rivers and hunt for fish and frogs.

They harvest crabs and shellfish from the bottom of rivers.

# Otter dens

A holt is an otter den. It is often well hidden under rocks or near tree roots.

Otters often creep out when it starts to get dark.

Otters must keep alert!

# Otter spotting

You might spot otters in an unspoilt habitat. This river bank might be good.

Keep still to avoid frightening the otters.

Good luck!

# Otter facts

Look: sleek brown fur, little ears

Skill: strong swimmers

Food: fish, frogs, crabs, shellfish

Den: holts

# Review: After reading

Use your assessment from hearing the children read to choose any GPCs, words or tricky words that need additional practice.

## Read 1: Decoding

- Model sounding out the following word, saying each of the sounds quickly and clearly. Then blend the sounds together.

  c/l/ear    clear

- Ask the children to say each of the sounds in the following words. How many sounds are there in each one?

  creep *(4)*            smart *(4)*            throat *(4)*

- Now ask the children if they can read each of the words without sounding them out.

## Read 2: Prosody

- Model reading each page with expression to the children.
- After you have read each page, ask the children to have a go at reading with expression.

## Read 3: Comprehension

- For every question ask the children how they know the answer. Ask:
  - What do otters eat? *(fish, frogs, crabs, shellfish)*
  - Can you remember the name of an otter's den? *(holt)*
  - What else did you learn about otters?

- Turn to pages 14 and 15 and look at the "Otter facts", asking the children to explain each fact in more detail, using the pages of the book for support.
- Discuss why otters might be difficult to spot. (e.g. *they prefer to come out at night, their holts are well hidden*)